MARK SIMPLIFIED

One Week, One Chapter

David Or

Doxa Abba Publishing

To my beloved wife and three sons,

*May we all seek to love Jesus more than
anything else in the world.*

CONTENTS

INTRODUCTION

I put this material together specifically for our youth group at Frisco Community Bible Church, and I'm really excited for you to dive into it! The way this devotional/discipleship material is designed is simple and manageable: you'll spend five days a week in prayer and reflection, meditating on God's Word. Don't worry —you've got two days off each week to rest or catch up if you need to. The key is to find the five days that work best for you, where you can sit down quietly, unplug from distractions, and enjoy intentional time with God.

I also added some modern images for each day, showing what it might be like if Jesus were here with us today. I hope these images bring you comfort and serve as a reminder that God's Word is just as alive and powerful now as it was when it was first written.

My heart in all of this is for you to learn to love Jesus more than anything else in the world. I truly believe that **the more we know God through His Word, the more we'll fall in love with Him.** As you go through the book of Mark, one chapter a week, I pray that God will reveal more of who He is to you. By the time you reach the end of this journey, I hope you'll feel closer to Jesus, not just in your head but in your heart. Let this be your space to grow, reflect, and experience His love in a deeper way. You've got this, and I'm praying for you along the way!

DAY 1 OF MARK 1: THE BEGINNING OF THE GOOD NEWS

Scripture References: Mark 1:1–8

Theme:
Mark opens with the declaration of the Gospel—the good news about Jesus, the Son of God. John the Baptist's ministry sets the stage for what is to come, calling people to repentance and preparing hearts for the arrival of the Messiah.

Bible Study Questions:

1. How does the opening of Mark shape your understanding of Jesus as the Son of God?

2. What does John the Baptist's message of repentance teach you about preparing your heart for God's work?

3. In what ways can you respond to the call for repentance in your own life?

Application:

Take a moment today to reflect on your personal journey of faith. Consider areas where you might need to "repent" or turn back to God, and commit to inviting Him to renew your heart.

Prayer Focus:

"Lord, thank You for the gift of Your Gospel. Help me prepare my heart each day to receive You with an open, repentant spirit. Amen."

DAY 2 OF MARK 1: BAPTISM AND OVERCOMING TEMPTATION

Scripture References: Mark 1:9–13

Theme:
Jesus' baptism marks the beginning of His public ministry and His identification with humanity. Following His baptism, He is tempted in the wilderness, showing us that even the Son of God faces challenges. This encourages us to trust in God's strength when we are tempted.

Bible Study Questions:

1. What significance does Jesus' baptism hold for understanding His identity and mission?

2. How does Jesus' experience with temptation speak to your own struggles?

3. What practical steps can you take to rely on God's strength when faced with temptation?

Application:
Reflect on a recent time when you faced a challenge or temptation. Consider how you can lean more on God's power in similar situations and seek His guidance through prayer or Scripture.

Prayer Focus:
"Jesus, thank You for showing me that even You faced temptation. Strengthen me to overcome my challenges and help me rely on Your power every day. Amen."

DAY 3 OF MARK 1: CALLED TO FOLLOW—LEAVING EVERYTHING BEHIND

Scripture References: Mark 1:16–20

Theme:
Jesus calls His first disciples—ordinary fishermen—to leave their nets and follow Him. This call is a powerful reminder that following Jesus often requires leaving behind old habits and embracing a new purpose centered on His mission.

Bible Study Questions:

1. What does the call to "follow me" mean to you personally?

2. How might you be holding on to habits or distractions that prevent you from fully following Jesus?

3. What changes are you willing to make in order to answer His call more completely?

Application:
Reflect on what "leaving everything behind" might look like in your own life. Identify one area—whether it's a habit, a relationship, or a routine—that you can adjust to make more room for following Jesus.

Prayer Focus:
"Lord, help me to follow You wholeheartedly. Give me the courage to leave behind what hinders my walk with You and embrace the new life You offer. Amen."

DAY 4 OF MARK 1: TEACHING WITH AUTHORITY AND DEMONSTRATING POWER

Scripture Referenes: Mark 1:21–28

Theme:
In the synagogue, Jesus amazes everyone with His teaching and His authority over unclean spirits. His words bring clarity and conviction, while His actions demonstrate that His power transcends earthly limits.

Bible Study Questions:

1. How does Jesus' teaching differ from the religious leaders of His time?

2. What does His authority over unclean spirits reveal about His power?

3. How can you invite the authority of Jesus into your own life, both in thought and in action?

Application:

Consider one area where you need clarity or freedom from negative influences. Ask God to help you embrace Jesus' authoritative teaching in that area and to empower you to live according to His truth.

Prayer Focus:

"Jesus, thank You for teaching with authority and showing Your power. Help me to embrace Your truth and live a life free from anything that opposes Your will. Amen."

DAY 5 OF MARK 1: COMPASSION IN ACTION—HEALING THE OUTCAST

Scripture References: Mark 1:40–45

Theme:
Moved by compassion, Jesus heals a man with leprosy, breaking social barriers and extending God's grace to an outcast. This act of mercy challenges us to reach out with kindness and love, regardless of societal norms or personal biases.

Bible Study Questions:

1. What does Jesus' willingness to heal a leper reveal about His heart for the marginalized?

2. How do societal norms sometimes prevent us from showing compassion to others?

3. In what practical ways can you show Christ-like compassion to those who are often overlooked?

Application:
Identify someone in your community who might be in need of a kind word, help, or a gesture of compassion. Make a plan to reach out in a way that demonstrates the love of Jesus.

Prayer Focus:
"Lord, thank You for Your boundless compassion. Help me to see others through Your eyes and to extend Your love and healing to everyone I meet. Amen."

DAY 1 OF MARK 2: FAITH THAT BREAKS THROUGH BARRIERS

Scripture References: Mark 2:1–4

Theme:
In this passage, Jesus is teaching in a crowded house when friends of a paralyzed man demonstrate extraordinary faith by lowering him through the roof. Their determined, creative action reminds us that true faith often involves community support and bold steps to overcome obstacles.

Bible Study Questions:

    1. What does the determination of the paralytic's friends

reveal about the nature of genuine faith?

2. How can you rely on and encourage others in your own journey of faith?

3. What "barriers" in your life might be overcome through the support of a caring community?

Application:
Today, think of one area where you feel stuck or challenged. Reach out to a trusted friend or small group for support, and consider how you might work together to break through obstacles, much like the friends who lowered the man through the roof.

Prayer Focus:
"Jesus, thank You for teaching me that faith is best lived out in community. Help me to be bold in seeking help and to encourage others to support one another in Your name. Amen."

DAY 2 OF MARK 2: FORGIVENESS AND HEALING—A NEW BEGINNING

Scripture References: Mark 2:5–12

Theme:
Jesus sees more than a physical need; He perceives the deeper spiritual need for forgiveness. By declaring the paralytic's sins forgiven and then healing him, Jesus shows that true healing begins with restoration of the heart and soul.

Bible Study Questions:

1. How does Jesus' willingness to forgive before healing the man challenge your understanding of true restoration?

2. In what ways have you experienced or witnessed the power of forgiveness leading to healing?

3. How can you allow Jesus' forgiveness to transform areas of hurt or brokenness in your life?

Application:
Reflect on any lingering hurts or burdens you might be carrying. Consider writing a prayer asking Jesus to forgive and restore your heart, and take a step toward letting go of past pain.

Prayer Focus:
"Lord, thank You for showing that forgiveness is the first step toward true healing. Cleanse my heart, restore my spirit, and help me to walk in the freedom of Your love. Amen."

DAY 3 OF MARK 2: CALLED TO FOLLOW —EMBRACING THE SINNER'S JOURNEY

Scripture References: Mark 2:13–14

Theme:
Jesus calls Levi, a tax collector, to follow Him—an invitation that upends societal expectations. This moment reminds us that Jesus seeks out those who are often overlooked or rejected, offering them a fresh start and a place at His table.

Bible Study Questions:

1. What does Levi's immediate response to Jesus' call tell you about the power of a personal encounter with Christ?

2. How does Jesus' invitation to Levi challenge societal norms about who is worthy of grace?

3. What might you need to leave behind in order to fully follow Jesus, as Levi did?

Application:
Take a moment to reflect on any areas of your life where you might feel unworthy or hesitant to follow Jesus. Consider embracing His call by taking one small step—perhaps a decision to serve in your community or deepen your study of Scripture.

Prayer Focus:
"Jesus, thank You for calling me, just as You called Levi. Help me to leave behind my old ways and step into the new life You offer with open arms and a grateful heart. Amen."

DAY 4 OF MARK 2: DINING WITH THE OUTCAST—A LESSON IN COMPASSION

Scripture References: Mark 2:15–17

Theme:
Jesus eats with tax collectors and sinners, provoking criticism from the religious leaders. His actions teach us that true compassion transcends social boundaries, inviting us to share in God's grace regardless of others' pasts.

Bible Study Questions:

1. How does Jesus' willingness to dine with sinners challenge cultural or personal prejudices you might hold?

2. In what ways does extending compassion to those who are different strengthen your own faith?

3. What practical steps can you take to reach out to someone who might feel excluded or judged?

Application:
Think about someone in your life or community who might feel marginalized or unworthy. Plan a simple act of kindness —whether it's an invitation to share a meal or a thoughtful conversation—to show them the inclusive love of Christ.

Prayer Focus:
"Lord, teach me to see others through Your eyes. Help me extend compassion and grace to everyone, especially those society may overlook. Amen."

DAY 5 OF MARK 2: NEW TRADITIONS FOR A NEW KINGDOM

Scripture References: Mark 2:18–22

Theme:
When questioned about fasting, Jesus uses the imagery of new wine in new wineskins to illustrate that His ministry brings a new way of living. Traditional practices must give way to fresh expressions of faith that are alive and dynamic.

Bible Study Questions:

1. What does the metaphor of new wine in new wineskins suggest about the changes Jesus is bringing?

2. How can you discern when it's time to adapt your spiritual practices to grow in your relationship with God?

3. In what areas of your faith life might you be holding on to old traditions that no longer serve your growth?

Application:

Reflect on your current spiritual disciplines and practices. Identify one habit that might need refreshing or replacing so that your faith can grow more vibrantly, just as new wine transforms its container.

Prayer Focus:

"Jesus, thank You for bringing new life and new ways to experience Your love. Help me to be open to change and to embrace fresh expressions of faith that honor You. Amen."

DAY 1 OF MARK 3: COMPASSION ON THE SABBATH

Scripture: Mark 3:1–6

Theme:
Jesus shows us that love and compassion should always come before rigid rules. His healing on the Sabbath reminds us that caring for others is more important than strict legalism.

Bible Study Questions:

1. What does Jesus' healing of the man with the shriveled hand reveal about His priorities?

2. How do you balance following rules with the need to show compassion in your everyday life?

3. Can you recall a time when showing kindness meant bending a rule or tradition for a greater good?

Application:
Think about one area in your life where a "rule" might be stopping you from reaching out to someone in need. This week, challenge yourself to choose compassion over perfection, just as Jesus did.

Prayer Focus:
"Lord, help me see beyond strict routines to the heart of Your compassion. Let me be a channel of Your love today. Amen."

DAY 2 OF MARK 3: WELCOMING THE MULTITUDE

Scripture: Mark 3:7–12

Theme:
Jesus doesn't keep His miracles private—He reaches out to everyone. When the crowds gathered, people experienced His healing and hope, reminding us that His love is available for all.

Bible Study Questions:

1. What does the gathering of the crowds tell you about people's need for hope and healing?

2. How does knowing that Jesus welcomes everyone influence the way you treat others?

3. What practical steps can you take this week to make sure others feel welcomed and cared for?

Application:
Look for ways to extend genuine hospitality or a kind word to someone who might be feeling left out. Sometimes, a simple "hello" or a listening ear can make all the difference.

Prayer Focus:
"Jesus, help me welcome others as You do—with open arms and a caring heart. Amen."

DAY 3 OF MARK 3: CALLED TO A SPECIAL PURPOSE

Scripture: Mark 3:13–19

Theme:
In choosing the twelve, Jesus shows that following Him is a calling. He invites ordinary people into an extraordinary mission—a reminder that each of us is called to be a part of His work.

Bible Study Questions:

1. What do you think it meant for Jesus to call people to be His disciples?

2. How does the appointment of the twelve inspire you to see your own unique role in God's mission?

3. What qualities in the disciples do you see reflected in your life or that you hope to cultivate?

Application:
Reflect on your personal journey of faith and consider one way you can actively participate in a community or ministry. Whether it's joining a small group or serving in a local outreach, every contribution matters.

Prayer Focus:
"Lord, thank You for calling me to be a part of Your mission. Guide me as I serve You and others with a willing heart. Amen."

DAY 4 OF MARK 3: RESPONDING TO CRITICISM WITH TRUTH

Scripture: Mark 3:22–30

Theme:
Not everyone understood Jesus' work. The accusations of the scribes remind us that sometimes doing what is right will attract criticism—but truth and love always prevail over misunderstanding.

Bible Study Questions:

1. Why do you think the scribes accused Jesus of being possessed by Beelzebul?

2. How does Jesus' response to these accusations inspire you to stand firm in the truth?

3. How can you respond to criticism or misunderstanding in a way that reflects Christ's love?

Application:
Consider an instance when you felt misunderstood or unfairly criticized. Ask God for the wisdom to respond with grace and truth, letting love lead your reactions.

Prayer Focus:
"Jesus, help me stand firm in Your truth and respond with grace even when I'm misunderstood. Amen."

DAY 5 OF MARK 3: FAMILY OF FAITH

Scripture: Mark 3:31–35

Theme:
Jesus redefines family—He calls those who do God's will His true family. This challenges us to see our community of believers as the family we choose and nurture.

Bible Study Questions:

1. What does it mean to be part of Jesus' family according to Mark 3:31–35?

2. How can you support and care for your spiritual family in practical ways?

3. In what ways does being part of God's family influence the way you live out your faith daily?

Application:
Reach out to a friend, neighbor, or fellow believer this week to encourage and support them. Sometimes, showing up for others is the best way to live out what it means to be in God's family.

Prayer Focus:
"Lord, help me to be a loving member of Your family. Teach me to care for others as You care for me every day. Amen."

DAY 1 OF MARK 4: THE PARABLE OF THE SOWER

Scripture: Mark 4:1–9

Theme:
Jesus uses the Parable of the Sower to show us that the condition of our hearts determines how well God's word takes root in our lives. Just as a farmer sows seeds, God shares His truth with us—but we must be ready to receive it.

Bible Study Questions:

1. What do you think each type of soil (the path, rocky ground, thorns, and good soil) represents in our

hearts?

2. How does this parable challenge you to examine the "soil" of your own heart?

3. In what ways can you cultivate "good soil" in your life to allow God's word to grow?

Application:
Reflect on your daily routine and attitudes. Consider one small change—like setting aside quiet time or journaling—that can help prepare your heart to receive God's truth more fully.

Prayer Focus:
"Jesus, help me be open and receptive to Your word. Clean my heart so that Your truth can grow in me each day. Amen."

DAY 2 OF MARK 4: UNDERSTANDING THE SOWER'S MESSAGE

Scripture: Mark 4:10–20

Theme:
In this passage, Jesus explains the meaning behind the parable. He reveals that the word of God is like a seed—its success depends on the condition of the listener's heart. Not everyone who hears will understand or accept it, but those who do can produce abundant fruit.

Bible Study Questions:

1. How does Jesus describe the different responses to the

word of God in this explanation?

2. What might "good soil" look like in your daily life?

3. How can you identify and remove obstacles that prevent your heart from growing in faith?

Application:
Take a few moments this week to reflect on what may be "choking" the growth of God's word in your life (such as worries, busyness, or distractions). Write them down and ask God for help in clearing them away.

Prayer Focus:
"Lord, help me to understand and embrace Your word. Remove the obstacles in my life so that Your truth can flourish in me. Amen."

DAY 3 OF MARK 4: THE LAMP AND THE LIGHT

Scripture: Mark 4:21–25

Theme:
Jesus teaches that His truth is not meant to be hidden—it's like a lamp that shines light for all to see. We're encouraged to let His word guide us openly and to share that light with others.

Bible Study Questions:

1. What does Jesus mean when He says that a lamp is meant to be placed on a stand?

2. How can you let the light of God shine through you in your everyday life?

3. What are some practical ways you can share the "light" of God with someone who is in darkness?

Application:
Think of one area where you can be more open about your faith. This week, choose a specific action—like inviting a friend to church or sharing a Bible verse—to let God's light shine through you.

Prayer Focus:
"Jesus, help me be a bright light for You. May I live openly and share Your love and truth with those around me. Amen."

DAY 4 OF MARK 4: THE PARABLE OF THE GROWING SEED

Scripture: Mark 4:26–29

Theme:
This parable shows that God's kingdom grows in mysterious ways—even when we can't see every step of the process. The growth of the seed is a reminder that God is always at work, even in moments when we feel uncertain or out of control.

Bible Study Questions:

1. How does the secret growth of the seed challenge your understanding of God's timing?

2. In what ways have you experienced God's work in your life that seemed mysterious or gradual?

3. How can you trust God more when you don't see immediate results from His work?

Application:
Reflect on a time when progress in your spiritual life felt slow or hidden. Remember that, like the seed, God's work is happening even when you can't see it. Write down a prayer of trust and patience.

Prayer Focus:
"Lord, help me trust Your process even when I can't see the results right away. I believe You are working in me, and I'm learning to be patient with Your timing. Amen."

DAY 5 OF MARK 4: THE MUSTARD SEED – A KINGDOM THAT GROWS

Scripture: Mark 4:30–32

Theme:
The mustard seed, though tiny, grows into something great and sheltering. This parable reminds us that God's kingdom may start small—in our hearts or communities—but with faith, it expands into something mighty that touches many lives.

Bible Study Questions:

1. What does the growth of the mustard seed reveal about God's power to transform even the smallest beginnings?

2. How can you nurture even the small seeds of faith in your life?

3. In what ways can your actions help God's kingdom grow in your community?

Application:
Identify one "small seed" of faith or an idea for ministry that you've been hesitant about. Take one small step this week to nurture that seed—whether it's starting a conversation, joining a group, or simply praying over it.

Prayer Focus:
"Jesus, thank You for the power of even the smallest seed. Help me nurture my faith and trust that You can grow something beautiful and mighty through me. Amen."

DAY 1 OF MARK 5: ENCOUNTER WITH A TORMENTED SOUL

Scripture References: Mark 5:1–5

Theme:
Jesus meets a man tormented by an unclean spirit in the region of the Gerasenes. This encounter reminds us that no one is beyond the reach of God's healing and that He sees the deepest struggles we face.

Bible Study Questions:

1. What can you learn from the way Jesus approached a man who was isolated by his torment?

2. How does knowing that Jesus cares for those in the depths of suffering encourage you in your own struggles?

3. In what ways might you be overlooking someone who needs Jesus' compassionate touch?

Application:
Reflect on someone in your life—perhaps someone who seems lost or deeply troubled—and consider one way you can show them kindness or offer support this week.

Prayer Focus:
"Jesus, help me recognize and reach out to those who feel isolated and tormented. Fill my heart with Your compassion so I can be a light in their darkness. Amen."

DAY 2 OF MARK 5: CONFRONTING DARKNESS WITH DIVINE AUTHORITY

Scripture References: Mark 5:6–13

Theme:
Jesus demonstrates His authority over the forces of evil by confronting and casting out the unclean spirits. This powerful act shows us that nothing is too strong for His power.

Bible Study Questions:

    1. What does Jesus' command over the unclean spirits

reveal about His power and authority?

2. How do you respond when faced with challenges that seem too overwhelming to overcome?

3. In what areas of your life do you need to invite Jesus' transformative power to break through darkness?

Application:
Consider one situation where fear or negativity has taken hold. Pray for courage and ask Jesus to bring His transformative power into that area, trusting that He can overcome all darkness.

Prayer Focus:
"Lord, remind me that You have authority over every dark and overwhelming situation. Help me trust in Your power to bring light and healing into my life. Amen."

DAY 3 OF MARK 5: A LIFE RESTORED AND A NEW MISSION

Scripture References: Mark 5:14–20

Theme:
After Jesus frees the man from his torment, the transformed individual is restored to his community and given a new mission—to share his testimony. His life becomes a living example of God's redeeming grace.

Bible Study Questions:

1. What changes in the man's life reflect the transformative work of Jesus?

2. How does being restored by God empower you to share His love with others?

3. What does it mean to you to be a living testimony of God's grace?

Application:
Think about how God has changed your life. Consider one practical way to share your story or a kind gesture that reflects the transformation He has worked in you.

Prayer Focus:
"Jesus, thank You for restoring my life and for giving me a purpose. Help me share the hope and transformation I have experienced with others every day. Amen."

DAY 4 OF MARK 5: A PLEA FOR HEALING AND AN ACT OF FAITH

Scripture References: Mark 5:21–34

Theme:
As Jesus continues His ministry, we see two intertwining stories: Jairus, a desperate leader pleading for the healing of his daughter, and a woman whose deep faith leads her to seek healing. Both accounts teach us about the power of faith and the importance of approaching Jesus with boldness.

Bible Study Questions:

1. How does Jairus' urgency in seeking Jesus' help inspire

your own prayers for healing or hope?

2. What does the woman's persistence in the midst of her suffering teach you about faith?

3. How can these stories encourage you to approach Jesus with your deepest needs and desires?

Application:
Identify an area in your life where you need healing or restoration. Approach that need with bold faith, knowing that Jesus welcomes you and is ready to help.

Prayer Focus:
"Lord, help me approach You with bold faith, trusting in Your power to heal and restore. May I never be afraid to ask for Your help when I need it most. Amen."

DAY 5 OF MARK 5: FROM DESPERATION TO MIRACULOUS RESTORATION

Scripture References: Mark 5:35–43

Theme:
In the climax of the chapter, Jesus brings life and hope where there was despair—raising Jairus' daughter and confirming the healing of the suffering woman. This miraculous restoration reminds us that Jesus is always working to bring new life and hope, even in our darkest moments.

Bible Study Questions:

1. What do the miracles of healing and restoration reveal about Jesus' compassion and power?

2. How does the story of Jairus' daughter encourage you to hope for new beginnings?

3. What does this account teach you about trusting in Jesus' timing and power?

Application:
Take a moment to reflect on areas in your life that need renewal. Write down a prayer of hope, trusting that Jesus is at work to bring new life and healing, even when you cannot see the full picture.

Prayer Focus:
"Jesus, thank You for turning desperation into hope and for bringing new life where there was none. Help me trust in Your perfect timing and power to restore and renew every part of my life. Amen."

DAY 1 OF MARK 6: REJECTION AND FAMILIAR FACES

Scripture References: Mark 6:1–6

Theme:
In His hometown, Jesus faces rejection by those who knew Him best. This passage challenges us to remember that familiarity can sometimes cloud our ability to see God's work in our midst.

Bible Study Questions:

1. What can we learn from the way Jesus was received in His own community?

2. How might familiarity with someone cause us to overlook their true value or message?

3. In what areas of your life do you struggle with taking things at face value rather than seeking deeper meaning?

Application:

Reflect on your own relationships and community. Consider one way you can approach someone or a situation with fresh eyes—acknowledging that God often works in unexpected ways.

Prayer Focus:

"Jesus, help me to see beyond the surface. Open my heart to recognize Your work in every person I meet, even when I think I already know them. Amen."

DAY 2 OF MARK 6:
SENT OUT TO SERVE

Scripture References: Mark 6:7–13

Theme:
Jesus commissions the Twelve, sending them out with authority and purpose. This call to service reminds us that God invites us to participate in His mission and to share His love with others.

Bible Study Questions:

1. What do you think the disciples learned from being sent out by Jesus?

2. How does this commissioning challenge you to consider your own role in God's mission?

3. What practical steps can you take to serve others in your community this week?

Application:
Identify a small, tangible way you can serve someone this week —whether it's offering a helping hand or sharing a kind word— and commit to doing it with a joyful heart.

Prayer Focus:
"Lord, thank You for calling me to serve. Guide my steps and fill me with courage as I share Your love with those around me. Amen."

DAY 3 OF MARK 6: CONTROVERSY AND OPPOSITION

Scripture References: Mark 6:14–29

Theme:
Jesus' growing fame brings controversy and criticism, even from powerful figures. Despite the opposition, Jesus remains focused on His mission, reminding us to stand firm in our faith regardless of external pressures.

Bible Study Questions:

1. How do the reactions of the authorities in this passage reveal the tension between truth and power?

2. What challenges do you face when your beliefs are met with skepticism or opposition?

3. How can you remain steadfast in your faith when confronted with criticism?

Application:
Think of a recent situation where you felt misunderstood or challenged because of your beliefs. Reflect on how you might respond with grace and firmness, just as Jesus did.

Prayer Focus:
"Jesus, help me stand strong in my faith. When I face opposition, let Your truth be my guide and Your love my response. Amen."

DAY 4 OF MARK 6: MIRACULOUS PROVISION

Scripture References: Mark 6:30–44

Theme:
The feeding of the five thousand demonstrates Jesus' compassion and His ability to provide abundantly, even from seemingly little resources. This miracle encourages us to trust that God can multiply our small acts of faith into something extraordinary.

Bible Study Questions:

1. What does this miracle teach you about God's ability to

provide in unexpected ways?

2. How might your small contributions be used by God to make a big difference?

3. In what areas of your life do you need to trust more in God's provision?

Application:

Consider one area in your life—be it time, talent, or resources —where you feel limited. Ask God to help you trust Him to multiply your efforts for His kingdom.

Prayer Focus:

"Lord, thank You for Your amazing provision. Help me to trust You with my small offerings, knowing You can turn them into something great. Amen."

DAY 5 OF MARK 6: STEPPING OUT IN FAITH

Scripture References: Mark 6:45–56

Theme:
After feeding the multitude, Jesus walks on water and calms the storm, inviting His disciples—and us—to step out in faith. This passage challenges us to overcome our fears and trust that Jesus is always with us, even in turbulent times.

Bible Study Questions:

1. What do you think the disciples learned when Jesus walked on water?

2. How does stepping out in faith change the way you face life's challenges?

3. What fears or doubts do you need to overcome in order to trust Jesus more fully?

Application:
Reflect on a current "storm" or challenge in your life. Consider taking one small step of faith today—whether it's reaching out for help, praying more intentionally, or simply trusting God's presence in the situation.

Prayer Focus:
"Jesus, help me to step out in faith even when the waves are high. Remind me that You are always with me, guiding and strengthening me through every storm. Amen.

DAY 1 OF MARK 7: BEYOND OUTWARD TRADITIONS

Scripture References: Mark 7:1–8

Theme:
Jesus challenges the focus on outward traditions over the inward heart. He shows that true worship comes from within, rather than simply following rituals or human-made customs.

Bible Study Questions:

1. What does Jesus' criticism of the Pharisees teach you about the importance of heart-based worship?

2. How might focusing solely on traditions limit our relationship with God?

3. In what ways can you shift your focus from external practices to internal transformation?

Application:

Take some time this week to examine your own practices. Is there an area where you've become overly focused on routine? Consider one intentional change to bring more heartfelt devotion into your daily life—perhaps through a quiet prayer or meditation time.

Prayer Focus:

"Lord, help me see past the rituals to the heart of true worship. Transform my inner life so that my actions reflect Your love and truth every day. Amen."

DAY 2 OF MARK 7: THE HEART OF WORSHIP

Scripture References: Mark 7:9–13

Theme:
Jesus warns against elevating human traditions above God's commands. He reminds us that true worship isn't about outward appearances but about honoring God from the heart.

Bible Study Questions:

1. How does Jesus' teaching in these verses challenge the way we prioritize traditions in our lives?

2. What dangers can arise when human customs override God's word?

3. How can you ensure that your daily worship comes from a sincere heart?

Application:
Reflect on any habits or routines that might be overshadowing your genuine relationship with God. Consider setting aside a specific time for honest prayer or journaling to connect with Him on a deeper level.

Prayer Focus:
"Jesus, help me align my heart with Yours. Teach me to value genuine worship over mere tradition, and let my life be a true expression of Your love. Amen."

DAY 3 OF MARK 7: INNER PURITY OVER EXTERNAL RITUALS

Scripture References: Mark 7:14–19

Theme:
Jesus emphasizes that what defiles a person is not what they eat but what comes out of their heart. This teaching challenges us to pursue inner purity and righteousness over mere external observance.

Bible Study Questions:

1. What do you think Jesus means by saying that external things do not defile a person?

2. How can the condition of your heart affect your relationship with God?

3. What practical steps can you take to cultivate inner purity and integrity?

Application:
Spend a moment in quiet reflection about the "voices" and influences in your life. Identify one area where you'd like to grow in inner purity—whether it's through forgiveness, self-reflection, or prayer—and commit to taking a small step in that direction this week.

Prayer Focus:
"Lord, cleanse my heart from anything that distances me from You. Help me focus on what truly matters and live a life that honors Your presence within me. Amen."

DAY 4 OF MARK 7: REDEFINING WHAT MATTERS

Scripture References: Mark 7:20–23

Theme:
Jesus teaches that what comes from the heart—such as evil thoughts, adultery, and other sins—shows the true source of defilement. This reminder calls us to reflect on our inner lives and prioritize what truly matters to God.

Bible Study Questions:

1. How does this teaching reshape your understanding of what defiles a person?

2. What inner attitudes or behaviors might need transformation in your own life?

3. How can you better guard your heart against the "evil thoughts" and actions that separate you from God?

Application:
Consider taking time this week to honestly evaluate your thoughts and actions. Perhaps keep a journal to record any negative patterns and pray for guidance in overcoming them. Small, consistent steps can lead to meaningful change.

Prayer Focus:
"Jesus, help me examine my heart and change the things that don't reflect Your goodness. Guide me toward thoughts and actions that bring me closer to You every day. Amen."

DAY 5 OF MARK 7: LIVING OUT A TRANSFORMED LIFE

Scripture References: Mark 7:24–30

Theme:
Jesus' encounter with the Syrophoenician woman, though later in the chapter, shows that transformation and inclusion go beyond cultural boundaries. This teaches us that a transformed heart reaches out in faith and compassion to everyone.

Bible Study Questions:

1. What does Jesus' interaction with the Syrophoenician woman reveal about the nature of true faith?

2. How can a transformed heart help break down barriers between different people or cultures?

3. In what ways can you share God's transformative love with someone who might be different from you?

Application:
Think of someone in your community who might feel excluded or misunderstood. Look for a way to reach out and show genuine care—whether through a kind word, an act of service, or simply listening to their story.

Prayer Focus:
"Lord, let my heart be transformed by Your love so that I may break down barriers and share Your compassion with everyone. Help me be a true ambassador of Your grace. Amen."

DAY 1 OF MARK 8: MIRACULOUS PROVISION FOR THE MULTITUDE

Scripture References: Mark 8:1–10

Theme:
In this passage, Jesus compassionately feeds the four thousand, demonstrating that He cares for the physical needs of the people and is able to provide abundantly—even when resources seem limited.

Bible Study Questions:

1. What does this miracle reveal about Jesus' heart for those who are hungry and in need?

2. How does witnessing God's provision encourage you to trust Him with your daily needs?

3. In what ways can you be a conduit of God's provision to someone else this week?

Application:
Reflect on a situation where you felt your resources were insufficient. Consider how God's miraculous provision might apply in that situation. Look for a small way to share what you have with someone else in need.

Prayer Focus:
"Jesus, thank You for showing me that You care about my needs. Help me trust in Your provision and use even my small resources to bless others. Amen."

DAY 2 OF MARK 8: RECOGNIZING SPIRITUAL BLINDNESS

Scripture References: Mark 8:11–21

Theme:
Jesus warns His disciples about the "leaven" of the Pharisees and Herod, challenging them to look beyond the visible and to seek spiritual understanding. This call invites us to examine our own hearts and discern between worldly concerns and the truth of God's Kingdom.

Bible Study Questions:

1. What might the "leaven" of the Pharisees and Herod

represent in our lives today?

2. How can focusing on worldly distractions hinder our spiritual vision?

3. What steps can you take to cultivate spiritual discernment and clarity?

Application:
Consider areas of your life where worldly concerns may be clouding your judgment. Choose one small practice—such as daily quiet time or a weekly review of your priorities—to help sharpen your spiritual focus.

Prayer Focus:
"Lord, help me see clearly amid the distractions of this world. Open my eyes to Your truth so I can live with wisdom and discernment. Amen."

DAY 3 OF MARK 8: A GRADUAL JOURNEY TO CLARITY

Scripture References: Mark 8:22–26

Theme:
In the healing of a blind man at Bethsaida, Jesus demonstrates that sometimes spiritual insight comes gradually. The process of healing reminds us that growth in faith and understanding can be progressive and transformative over time.

Bible Study Questions:

1. How does the gradual healing of the blind man speak to the process of spiritual growth in your life?

2. What challenges have you faced in moving from confusion to clarity in your faith?

3. How can you nurture patience as you trust God to open your eyes to His truth?

Application:
Reflect on an area in your spiritual life where progress has been slow. Commit to being patient and persistent in prayer and Bible study, trusting that God is working to bring clarity and transformation.

Prayer Focus:
"Jesus, thank You for working slowly yet surely in my life. Help me to be patient and persistent as You open my eyes to Your truth. Amen."

DAY 4 OF MARK 8: A BOLD CONFESSION OF FAITH

Scripture References: Mark 8:27–30

Theme:
Peter's confession—declaring Jesus as the Christ—marks a pivotal moment in the disciples' journey. This recognition invites us to boldly proclaim our faith and to acknowledge Jesus' true identity as our Savior and Lord.

Bible Study Questions:

    1. What significance does Peter's confession hold for your understanding of who Jesus is?

2. How can recognizing Jesus as the Christ transform the way you live daily?

3. In what practical ways can you share your confession of faith with those around you?

Application:
Take time to reflect on your personal journey with Jesus. Consider sharing your testimony with a friend or writing it down as a reminder of His transformative power in your life.

Prayer Focus:
"Lord, thank You for revealing Yourself to me. Help me to boldly proclaim that You are my Savior and guide my words and actions as I live out my faith. Amen."

DAY 5 OF MARK 8: THE COST AND CALL OF DISCIPLESHIP

Scripture References: Mark 8:31–38

Theme:
In this powerful passage, Jesus speaks about His impending suffering and death and calls His followers to deny themselves, take up their cross, and follow Him. This teaching challenges us to consider the true cost of discipleship and the importance of living a life fully surrendered to God.

Bible Study Questions:

　　1. What does Jesus' prediction about His suffering teach

you about the nature of His mission?

2. How does the call to deny oneself challenge your current lifestyle and priorities?

3. What changes might you need to make to more fully follow Jesus, even when it requires sacrifice?

Application:
Reflect on areas of your life where self-interest may be hindering your discipleship. Identify one specific action you can take to align more closely with Jesus' call—whether it's giving up a habit, changing a priority, or serving someone in need.

Prayer Focus:
"Jesus, help me to take up my cross and follow You with all my heart. Teach me to live a life of sacrifice and service, trusting in Your plan above my own. Amen."

DAY 1 OF MARK 9: A GLIMPSE OF DIVINE GLORY

Scripture References: Mark 9:2–8

Theme:
In the Transfiguration, Jesus reveals His divine glory to Peter, James, and John. This moment shows us that there is a deeper, radiant reality beyond our everyday experiences—a promise of transformation for those who follow Him.

Bible Study Questions:

> 1. What do you think the disciples felt when they saw Jesus transfigured before them?

2. How does this glimpse of Jesus' glory encourage you to trust in His power in your life?

3. What does the idea of transformation mean to you personally?

Application:
Take some time today to reflect on moments when you've experienced unexpected brightness or hope in your life. Consider keeping a journal entry about these moments and how they remind you of Jesus' glory and transformative power.

Prayer Focus:
"Jesus, thank You for showing me Your glory. Help me to see beyond my everyday struggles and trust that You are transforming my life in ways I might not always understand. Amen."

DAY 2 OF MARK 9: RESPONDING TO REVELATION

Scripture References: Mark 9:9–13

Theme:
After the Transfiguration, Jesus instructs His disciples not to share what they had seen until the proper time. This teaches us about the value of experiencing God's truth personally before we share it with the world.

Bible Study Questions:

1. Why do you think Jesus asked His disciples to keep the Transfiguration a secret for a time?

2. How can you discern when to share your spiritual experiences and when to hold them close as personal growth?

3. In what ways can a deeper personal encounter with God strengthen your testimony?

Application:
Reflect on a time when you experienced a clear moment of God's presence. Consider how that personal encounter has shaped your life, and think about ways you might deepen that experience through quiet reflection or prayer.

Prayer Focus:
"Lord, help me to treasure my personal encounters with You. Guide me in knowing when to speak and when to quietly grow in my faith, trusting in Your perfect timing. Amen."

DAY 3 OF MARK 9: A LESSON IN FAITH AND PERSISTENCE

Scripture References: Mark 9:14–29

Theme:
In the healing of the boy with an unclean spirit, Jesus teaches us about the power of persistent faith. Both the desperate father and the boy's experience remind us that even when our faith seems small or our challenges great, Jesus is ready to bring healing.

Bible Study Questions:

    1. What does the father's plea for his son's healing reveal

about his faith?

2. How do you react when you face situations that test your patience or belief?

3. What steps can you take to nurture and grow your faith during difficult times?

Application:
Think about an area in your life where you're facing a challenge or doubt. Consider taking a small step of faith—whether that's praying for guidance, reaching out for support, or simply trusting God a little more—and notice how that changes your perspective.

Prayer Focus:
"Jesus, thank You for hearing my desperate prayers. Help me to be persistent in my faith and to trust that You are working, even when I can't see the full picture. Amen."

DAY 4 OF MARK 9: EMBRACING HUMILITY AND SERVICE

Scripture References: Mark 9:33–37

Theme:
When the disciples argue about who is the greatest, Jesus teaches them that true greatness comes through humility and serving others. This reminder challenges us to value service and kindness over status and recognition.

Bible Study Questions:

1. How does Jesus' teaching on humility challenge common ideas about success and greatness?

2. In what ways can you practice humility in your everyday interactions?

3. How can you serve those around you without expecting recognition or reward?

Application:
Look for a small, practical opportunity this week to serve someone—whether it's a kind word, a helping hand, or a listening ear. Notice how these acts of service bring you closer to the heart of Jesus' teaching on humility.

Prayer Focus:
"Lord, help me to be humble and serve others selflessly. May my actions reflect Your love and lead me to a deeper understanding of true greatness in Your kingdom. Amen."

DAY 5 OF MARK 9: GUARDING AGAINST TEMPTATION AND EMBRACING PURITY

Scripture References: Mark 9:42–50

Theme:
In His stern warnings about causing others to stumble and the seriousness of sin, Jesus reminds us of the importance of guarding our hearts and lives. This call to purity is not about legalism, but about protecting the well-being of our faith community and our personal walk with God.

Bible Study Questions:

1. What do Jesus' warnings about sin teach you about the impact of your actions on others?

2. How can you actively work to guard your heart against temptations that lead you away from God?

3. In what ways can you encourage and support others in maintaining a pure and honest relationship with God?

Application:
Identify one habit or influence in your life that might be pulling you away from your commitment to God. Consider a concrete step you can take to reduce that influence—whether it's changing a routine or seeking support from a trusted friend or mentor.

Prayer Focus:
"Jesus, help me protect my heart and mind from anything that could lead me away from You. Guide me in living a life that honors You and supports the faith of those around me. Amen."

DAY 1 OF MARK 10: GOD'S DESIGN FOR MARRIAGE

Scripture References: Mark 10:1–12

Theme:
Jesus teaches about the sacred bond of marriage, emphasizing that it was designed to be a lifelong commitment. His words challenge us to value and honor our relationships according to God's original plan.

Bible Study Questions:

1. What does Jesus' teaching on marriage reveal about God's intention for the relationship between a husband

and wife?

2. How might modern views on relationships conflict with the way Jesus describes marriage?

3. What practical steps can you take to strengthen your own relationships or support those in committed relationships?

Application:
Reflect on your own relationships—whether you're married, dating, or supporting others. Consider one concrete way you can honor and nurture those bonds, such as setting aside quality time or offering heartfelt encouragement.

Prayer Focus:
"Lord, thank You for designing marriage as a beautiful, lifelong bond. Help me honor and nurture the relationships in my life, reflecting Your love and commitment every day. Amen."

DAY 2 OF MARK 10: RECEIVING THE KINGDOM LIKE A CHILD

Scripture References: Mark 10:13–16

Theme:
Jesus welcomes little children and reminds us that entering His kingdom requires childlike faith—simple, trusting, and open. His invitation is for everyone, regardless of age or status.

Bible Study Questions:

    1. What does Jesus' attitude toward children teach you

about the kind of faith He values?

2. How can you cultivate a more open, trusting heart like that of a child?

3. In what ways can you help create an environment that welcomes others with a similar spirit of simplicity and trust?

Application:

Think of one area where you might be overcomplicating your faith. Choose to approach that area with the openness and trust of a child—perhaps by simplifying your prayer life or by sharing your faith in a genuine, unguarded way.

Prayer Focus:

"Jesus, thank You for welcoming me as You welcomed the children. Teach me to trust You with a simple, open heart and to invite others to experience Your love in the same way. Amen."

DAY 3 OF MARK 10: THE CHALLENGE OF WEALTH AND THE RICH YOUNG RULER

Scripture References: Mark 10:17–31

Theme:
Jesus encounters the rich young ruler, who struggles with the demands of following Him due to his attachment to wealth. This encounter challenges us to examine our priorities and trust God above material possessions.

Bible Study Questions:

1. What does the interaction between Jesus and the rich young ruler teach you about the cost of discipleship?

2. How might material wealth hinder a deeper relationship with God?

3. What steps can you take to realign your priorities, placing God and His kingdom above worldly possessions?

Application:
Take a moment to review your own life and resources. Identify one area—whether it's time, money, or attention—where you might be overly attached to material things, and consider a small step to reorient your focus toward God's eternal promises.

Prayer Focus:
"Lord, help me see that true treasure is found in following You. Guide me to place my trust and focus on Your kingdom rather than on earthly wealth. Amen."

DAY 4 OF MARK 10: EMBRACING THE COST OF DISCIPLESHIP AND SERVANTHOOD

Scripture References: Mark 10:32–45

Theme:
Jesus predicts His own suffering and redefines greatness as servanthood. He calls us to deny ourselves and take up our cross, challenging us to live lives of humility, sacrifice, and service to others.

Bible Study Questions:

1. What does Jesus mean when He says that true greatness is found in serving others?

2. How does the call to take up one's cross change the way you view your daily responsibilities?

3. In what practical ways can you serve those around you, following Jesus' example of humility and sacrifice?

Application:
Consider an opportunity this week to serve someone in need—a neighbor, a friend, or a community member. Let this act of service remind you of Jesus' call to live selflessly, even when it means stepping out of your comfort zone.

Prayer Focus:
"Jesus, thank You for showing me that true greatness comes through service. Help me to embrace the challenges of discipleship with a willing heart and to serve others with love and humility. Amen."

DAY 5 OF MARK 10: COMPASSION ON THE ROAD TO HEALING

Scripture References: Mark 10:46–52

Theme:
In the healing of blind Bartimaeus, Jesus demonstrates both compassion and power. Bartimaeus's bold faith and persistent cry for help remind us that Jesus hears our pleas and is ready to restore us, even when we feel unseen.

Bible Study Questions:

1. What does Bartimaeus's persistence teach you about seeking Jesus in times of need?

2. How does Jesus' willingness to stop and help a marginalized individual encourage you in your own struggles?

3. What can you learn from this story about the importance of faith when approaching Jesus for healing or help?

Application:
Reflect on a personal challenge where you long for healing or restoration. Consider reaching out to Jesus in prayer with the same boldness as Bartimaeus, trusting that He will meet you in your need.

Prayer Focus:
"Lord, thank You for Your compassion and power to heal. Help me to call out to You with bold faith, knowing that You are always there to restore and guide me. Amen."

DAY 1 OF MARK 11: WELCOMING THE KING

Scripture References: Mark 11:1–10

Theme:
Jesus' triumphant entry into Jerusalem shows us what it means to welcome God as King. The crowd's joyful celebration and recognition of His authority remind us that honoring Jesus begins with a willing, expectant heart.

Bible Study Questions:

1. What does the crowd's response to Jesus' entry teach you about recognizing His kingship?

2. How can you welcome Jesus into your daily life, just as the people welcomed Him on that day?

3. What might it look like to honor Jesus as King in both your small routines and big decisions?

Application:
Today, take a moment to invite Jesus into your day. Whether through a quiet morning prayer or setting an intention for how you'll act, consciously welcome Him as the King of your heart and life.

Prayer Focus:
"Jesus, thank You for coming into my life as my King. Help me welcome You each day with open arms and a joyful heart. Amen."

DAY 2 OF MARK 11: LESSONS FROM THE WITHERING FIG TREE

Scripture References: Mark 11:12–14

Theme:
In the story of the withering fig tree, Jesus uses a powerful visual to teach about the importance of bearing fruit. The tree's sudden loss of life challenges us to examine our own lives for genuine growth and fruitfulness.

Bible Study Questions:

1. What does the withering fig tree symbolize in terms of our personal spiritual growth?

2. How might neglecting spiritual fruit lead to consequences in our lives?

3. What steps can you take to ensure that your life is bearing the fruit of faith and good works?

Application:
Reflect on areas of your life that may feel unproductive or barren. Consider one practical change—like dedicating more time for prayer, reflection, or service—to nurture growth and bear lasting fruit.

Prayer Focus:
"Lord, help me cultivate a life full of fruit. Remove any areas of neglect so that I may grow in Your love and purpose every day. Amen."

DAY 3 OF MARK 11: CLEANSING THE TEMPLE: A CALL TO PURE WORSHIP

Scripture References: Mark 11:15–19

Theme:
When Jesus cleanses the temple, He demonstrates that true worship is not about commerce or empty rituals but about reverence, purity, and a sincere connection with God. His actions challenge us to evaluate what we allow in our hearts and lives.

Bible Study Questions:

1. How does Jesus' cleansing of the temple encourage you to pursue genuine worship?

2. What "clutter" might be interfering with your relationship with God?

3. How can you create a personal space—physically or spiritually—that reflects a pure, undistracted heart for God?

Application:
Take time today to reflect on any habits or influences that distract you from authentic worship. Consider decluttering your environment or your schedule, making space for quiet moments with God.

Prayer Focus:
"Jesus, help me clear away anything that distracts me from truly worshiping You. Purify my heart and guide me toward a life of sincere devotion. Amen."

DAY 4 OF MARK 11: THE AUTHORITY OF CHRIST IN OUR LIVES

Scripture References: Mark 11:20–25

Theme:
After witnessing the events of the day, Jesus teaches about the power of faith and the authority given to believers in prayer. His words remind us that when we trust in Him, even seemingly impossible challenges can be overcome.

Bible Study Questions:

1. What does Jesus' teaching on faith and authority reveal about the power available to believers?

2. How can you apply this truth when facing obstacles or challenges in your life?

3. In what ways can your prayers reflect trust in Jesus' authority and power?

Application:
Think about a current challenge or a situation that feels overwhelming. Pray with confidence, trusting that Jesus' authority is at work in your life. Write down a specific prayer request and commit to praying over it regularly.

Prayer Focus:
"Lord, thank You for the authority You've given me through faith. Strengthen my trust in Your power, and help me to pray boldly and confidently. Amen."

DAY 5 OF MARK 11: LIVING IN THE PRESENCE OF THE KING

Scripture References: Mark 11 (Reflect on the entirety of the chapter)

Theme:
Mark 11 as a whole invites us to live with an awareness of Jesus' authority—from the joyful welcome at His entry to the cleansing of the temple and the lessons on faith. When we live in His presence, every aspect of our lives reflects His love and truth.

Bible Study Questions:

1. How do the events in Mark 11 collectively reveal Jesus' character and authority?

2. What does it mean to live each day aware of Jesus' presence as King in your life?

3. How can you ensure that your daily actions reflect the lessons learned from this chapter?

Application:
Spend a few minutes today reviewing your day and considering how you recognized or missed opportunities to honor Jesus' presence. Set an intention for tomorrow to be more mindful of His guidance in every moment.

Prayer Focus:
"Jesus, help me live each day in the reality of Your presence. Guide my thoughts, actions, and decisions so that I may honor You as my King. Amen."

DAY 1 OF MARK 12: THE PARABLE OF THE WICKED TENANTS

Scripture References: Mark 12:1–12

Theme:
Jesus tells the parable of the wicked tenants to reveal how God entrusts His kingdom to people—but some refuse to honor that trust. This story invites us to reflect on how we receive and steward God's blessings in our own lives.

Bible Study Questions:

1. What does the parable teach you about the responsibilities that come with God's gifts?

2. How can the idea of faithful stewardship apply to your daily actions?

3. In what ways might you be tempted to take God's blessings for granted, and how can you change that?

Application:
Spend some time today reviewing how you use the gifts and opportunities God has given you—whether in your work, relationships, or personal growth. Choose one area to improve as an act of faithful stewardship.

Prayer Focus:
"Lord, help me be a faithful steward of all You have entrusted to me. Open my eyes to see every blessing as a responsibility to honor You in all I do. Amen."

DAY 2 OF MARK 12: BALANCING EARTHLY AND HEAVENLY OBLIGATIONS

Scripture References: Mark 12:13–17

Theme:
When questioned about paying taxes, Jesus shows us how to navigate the tension between earthly obligations and our ultimate loyalty to God. His answer encourages us to live with integrity in both realms.

Bible Study Questions:

1. What does Jesus' response about taxes reveal about balancing worldly duties with spiritual priorities?

2. How do you navigate situations where earthly demands conflict with your faith?

3. In what practical ways can you honor God while fulfilling your responsibilities in society?

Application:
Reflect on an area in your life where you face a conflict between worldly expectations and your spiritual values. Think of one action you can take to ensure that your decisions honor God first.

Prayer Focus:
"Jesus, guide me in balancing my daily responsibilities with my commitment to You. Help me honor You in every decision I make. Amen."

DAY 3 OF MARK 12: UNDERSTANDING THE RESURRECTION AND ETERNAL LIFE

Scripture References: Mark 12:18–27

Theme:
In this passage, Jesus addresses questions about the resurrection. His teaching invites us to shift our perspective from the temporary to the eternal, encouraging us to live with hope in the promise of life beyond this world.

Bible Study Questions:

1. How does Jesus' teaching on the resurrection shape your understanding of eternal life?

2. What impact does the promise of resurrection have on your daily struggles or fears?

3. In what ways can you live more fully in the hope of eternal life today?

Application:
Take a few moments to reflect on the hope that comes from Jesus' promise of resurrection. Let that hope comfort you and guide your actions, especially during challenging times.

Prayer Focus:
"Lord, thank You for the hope of resurrection and eternal life. Fill my heart with that hope so I may face each day with courage and trust in Your promises. Amen."

DAY 4 OF MARK 12: THE GREATEST COMMANDMENT: LOVE GOD AND LOVE OTHERS

Scripture References: Mark 12:28–34

Theme:
Jesus sums up the Law by emphasizing that loving God with all your heart and loving your neighbor are the two greatest commandments. This teaching challenges us to let love be the driving force behind our every action.

Bible Study Questions:

1. What does it mean to love God with all your heart, soul, mind, and strength?

2. How can loving your neighbor transform both your life and your community?

3. What are some practical ways you can demonstrate this kind of love daily?

Application:

Identify one relationship or community need that you can serve in a tangible way this week. Let your actions reflect the deep love that Jesus calls us to show for both God and others.

Prayer Focus:

"Jesus, help me love You with everything I have and extend that love to everyone around me. Teach me to live a life filled with compassion, kindness, and genuine care. Amen."

DAY 5 OF MARK 12: WHO IS THE CHRIST? A CALL TO REFLECT ON JESUS' IDENTITY

Scripture References: Mark 12:35–37

Theme:
Jesus challenges us with questions about His identity—inviting us to ponder what it truly means for Him to be the Son of God. This passage calls us to deepen our understanding of who Jesus is and what that means for our lives.

Bible Study Questions:

1. How do you personally understand the identity of Jesus as the Son of God?

2. What implications does this identity have for the way you live and make decisions?

3. In what ways can you grow in your understanding of Jesus' nature and purpose?

Application:
Spend some time reflecting on your own beliefs about who Jesus is. Consider reading further or discussing with a friend or mentor how His identity transforms your daily life. Let this reflection inspire you to live more intentionally for Him.

Prayer Focus:
"Lord, open my eyes to who You truly are. Deepen my understanding of Your identity as the Son of God, and help me live each day in the light of Your truth. Amen."

DAY 1 OF MARK 13: RECOGNIZING THE SIGNS OF THE TIMES

Scripture References: Mark 13:1–8

Theme:
Jesus begins His Olivet Discourse by describing signs of coming troubles—wars, earthquakes, and other upheavals—that signal the beginning of the end times. These verses encourage us to remain watchful and discerning, understanding that while challenges will arise, God remains in control.

Bible Study Questions:

1. What signs does Jesus mention that indicate the

beginning of these events, and how do they relate to our world today?

2. How can being aware of these signs help you focus on God rather than fear?

3. What does it mean to be "watchful" in your personal walk of faith?

Application:
Take a moment to reflect on how you stay alert to God's work amid life's chaos. Consider setting aside a few minutes each day for quiet reflection or journaling about how the events in your life point you back to God.

Prayer Focus:
"Jesus, help me to see Your guiding hand in the midst of uncertainty. Teach me to remain watchful and focused on You, trusting that You are in control. Amen."

DAY 2 OF MARK 13: STANDING FIRM THROUGH PERSECUTION

Scripture References: Mark 13:9–13

Theme:
Jesus warns that His followers will face persecution, rejection, and even betrayal. Yet He also assures us that the Spirit will guide us during these times. This passage encourages believers to stand firm in their faith, knowing that enduring trials refines our trust in God.

Bible Study Questions:

1. How does Jesus describe the nature of persecution that His followers will face?

2. In what ways has your faith been tested by opposition or hardship?

3. What practical steps can you take to remain grounded in the Spirit when facing difficulties?

Application:
Think of a recent challenge where you felt tested in your faith. Identify one positive action—such as joining a small group, praying with a friend, or reading Scripture—that can bolster your spirit during tough times.

Prayer Focus:
"Lord, give me strength and courage when I face opposition. Help me stand firm in my faith and trust in Your guidance through every trial. Amen."

DAY 3 OF MARK 13: STAYING ROOTED AMID DECEPTION

Scripture References: Mark 13:14–23

Theme:

Jesus warns about the "abomination of desolation" and the rise of false prophets who will try to mislead many. This passage calls us to remain rooted in the truth of God's word, keeping our focus on what is genuine rather than being swayed by deceptive appearances.

Bible Study Questions:

    1. What do you think Jesus means by "the abomination of

desolation," and how does that warning apply today?

2. How can you distinguish between true guidance and deceptive messages in your daily life?

3. What practices can help you stay grounded in the truth of God's word?

Application:
Examine your sources of information and influences—both spiritual and secular. Consider committing to a regular time of Bible reading or devotional study to reinforce your understanding of God's truth.

Prayer Focus:
"Jesus, help me to discern truth from deception. Keep me rooted in Your word so that I may navigate life's challenges with clarity and wisdom. Amen."

DAY 4 OF MARK 13: THE PROMISE OF HIS GLORIOUS RETURN

Scripture References: Mark 13:24–27

Theme:
Jesus describes His return in glory—a cosmic event that will signal the full realization of God's kingdom. These verses inspire hope and remind us that despite the trials we face now, a glorious future awaits all who trust in Him.

Bible Study Questions:

1. How does the promise of Jesus' return shape your hope for the future?

2. In what ways do you find comfort in knowing that Jesus will gather His elect?

3. How does this promise affect the way you live today, especially when facing difficulties?

Application:
Reflect on the hope that comes from Jesus' promise of a glorious return. Write down or share with someone one hope or promise from this passage that inspires you, and let that hope guide your daily actions.

Prayer Focus:
"Lord, thank You for the promise of Your return and the hope it brings. Fill my heart with joy and anticipation as I live each day in the light of Your eternal glory. Amen."

DAY 5 OF MARK 13: LIVING IN CONSTANT READINESS

Scripture References: Mark 13:28–37

Theme:
Jesus concludes His discourse by urging His followers to be constantly watchful, for no one knows the exact day or hour of His return. This call to vigilance reminds us to live each day with purpose, being ready to meet Him at any moment.

Bible Study Questions:

1. What does it mean to be "watchful" in the context of Jesus' teachings in this passage?

2. How can you incorporate a mindset of readiness into your daily routines?

3. What changes might you make in your life to live with greater urgency and purpose for God?

Application:
Review your daily habits and priorities. Identify one small change—like starting your day with prayer or setting aside time for reflection—that can help you stay alert and spiritually prepared for whenever Jesus may return.

Prayer Focus:
"Jesus, help me live each day with a spirit of readiness and purpose. May I always be prepared to welcome You with an open heart and a vigilant mind. Amen."

DAY 1 OF MARK 14: THE PLOT AGAINST JESUS AND A TOUCH OF HONOR

Scripture References: Mark 14:1–11

Theme:
As the religious leaders plot against Jesus, a woman anoints Him with costly perfume—a bold act of devotion in the face of impending betrayal. This juxtaposition reminds us that even amid dark times, genuine worship and honor for Christ shine through.

Bible Study Questions:

1. What does the contrast between the leaders' secret plot and the woman's public act of devotion reveal about different responses to Jesus?

2. How might an act of sincere worship challenge the status quo in your own life?

3. In what ways can you honor Jesus with something valuable—even when others may not understand your devotion?

Application:
Reflect on what you value most. Consider one intentional act of worship or generosity you can offer to honor Jesus this week, even if it goes against popular opinion.

Prayer Focus:
"Lord, thank You for showing me that true worship comes from a sincere heart. Help me honor You boldly, even when it's not popular, and guide me to use my gifts for Your glory. Amen."

DAY 2 OF MARK 14: THE LAST SUPPER AND THE NEW COVENANT

Scripture References: Mark 14:12–26

Theme:
At the Last Supper, Jesus gathers His disciples and institutes the Lord's Supper, establishing a new covenant of grace and forgiveness. This moment invites us to remember His sacrifice and to share in the hope of redemption.

Bible Study Questions:

1. How does the imagery of the bread and wine deepen your understanding of Jesus' sacrifice?

2. In what ways does the Last Supper remind you of the new covenant and promise of forgiveness?

3. How can you live out the truth of this new covenant in your everyday interactions with others?

Application:
Spend time in reflection on the significance of communion in your life. Consider how you can more intentionally remember and share the hope of Jesus' sacrifice with those around you—perhaps through a shared meal or a personal conversation.

Prayer Focus:
"Jesus, thank You for the gift of Your body and blood, given for my redemption. Help me live in the light of Your new covenant and share the hope of Your forgiveness with everyone I meet. Amen."

DAY 3 OF MARK 14: A WARNING OF WEAKNESS AND A CALL TO VIGILANCE

Scripture References: Mark 14:27–31

Theme:
Jesus predicts His disciples' falling away—even Peter's denial—revealing our human frailty and need for grace. His honest warning encourages us to remain vigilant, humble, and dependent on God's strength.

Bible Study Questions:

1. What does Jesus' prediction about His disciples reveal about the nature of human weakness?

2. How does recognizing your own vulnerability help you lean more fully on God's grace?

3. In what practical ways can you build spiritual resilience to withstand moments of weakness?

Application:
Reflect on a time when you fell short despite your best efforts. Allow that memory to remind you of the importance of God's grace and commit to seeking His strength through prayer, fellowship, or Scripture.

Prayer Focus:
"Lord, thank You for Your honest words that reveal my need for You. Strengthen me in my moments of weakness and help me rely on Your grace each day. Amen."

DAY 4 OF MARK 14: AGONY IN THE GARDEN

Scripture References: Mark 14:32–42

Theme:
In the Garden of Gethsemane, Jesus prays with deep anguish, expressing His struggle as He faces the weight of what is to come. His vulnerable, honest prayer teaches us the importance of surrendering our fears and desires to God's will.

Bible Study Questions:

1. How does Jesus' prayer in the garden encourage you to be honest with God about your struggles?

2. What does His example teach you about surrendering to God's will even when it is painful?

3. In what ways can you create a space for honest, vulnerable prayer in your own life?

Application:
Set aside a quiet moment today to be completely honest with God about your fears and challenges. Write down your prayers and desires, then ask for His guidance to align your will with His.

Prayer Focus:
"Jesus, thank You for sharing Your heart with me in Your darkest hour. Help me to surrender my fears and trust in Your perfect will, no matter how hard the path may be. Amen."

DAY 5 OF MARK 14: BETRAYAL, ARREST, AND THE COST OF DISCIPLESHIP

Scripture References: Mark 14:43–72

Theme:
As Jesus is betrayed and arrested, we see the painful cost of following Him, highlighted by Peter's denial. This day reminds us that while human failure is real, God's forgiveness and restoration are always available to those who repent and seek Him.

Bible Study Questions:

1. How does the betrayal and arrest of Jesus challenge your understanding of loyalty and sacrifice?

2. What lessons can you learn from Peter's denial about the pitfalls of fear and human frailty?

3. How can you experience and extend God's forgiveness when you fall short in your walk of faith?

Application:
Reflect on moments when you have failed to live up to your calling. Consider taking one step to seek reconciliation —whether through personal prayer, reaching out to someone you've hurt, or embracing God's forgiveness more fully in your own life.

Prayer Focus:
"Lord, thank You for Your boundless forgiveness even when I fail. Help me to learn from my mistakes, lean on Your mercy, and stand firm in the cost of following You. Amen."

DAY 1 OF MARK 15: THE TRIAL BEFORE PILATE

Scripture References: Mark 15:1–15

Theme:
Jesus is brought before Pilate as the religious leaders press their accusations. Despite the injustice and false charges, Jesus remains silent and composed. This passage challenges us to consider how we respond to unfair treatment and to trust God's ultimate justice.

Bible Study Questions:

1. What does Jesus' calm and silent demeanor in the

face of false accusations teach you about handling injustice?

2. How do you react when you feel misunderstood or wrongly accused in your own life?

3. In what ways can trusting in God's justice help you face challenging situations?

Application:
Reflect on a time when you felt unfairly treated. Consider how you might respond with patience and trust in God's timing, rather than seeking immediate retribution. Write down one prayer or action step to help you lean on God's strength during such moments.

Prayer Focus:
"Lord, when I feel misunderstood or wronged, help me to trust in Your justice and remain calm like Jesus. Give me strength to respond with grace and faith. Amen."

DAY 2 OF MARK 15: THE MOCKERY AND SCORN

Scripture References: Mark 15:16–20

Theme:
Jesus is mocked and ridiculed by soldiers and onlookers as He is led away. Despite the harsh treatment and abuse, Jesus' dignity and purpose remain intact. This passage invites us to reflect on how we maintain our integrity and compassion even when facing ridicule.

Bible Study Questions:

1. How does Jesus' response to mockery challenge you to handle

criticism or scorn in your own life?

2. What lessons can be learned from the way Jesus maintained His dignity amid abuse?

3. How can you support others who are being ridiculed or mistreated?

Application:
Think of someone (or even a personal experience) where mockery or harsh words were involved. Reflect on how you can offer support or choose to respond with kindness and integrity instead of bitterness.

Prayer Focus:
"Jesus, help me to keep my dignity and extend grace even when I or others face ridicule. May I always reflect Your love and strength. Amen."

DAY 3 OF MARK 15: THE WEIGHT OF THE CROSS

Scripture References: Mark 15:21–32

Theme:
Simon of Cyrene is compelled to help carry the cross, symbolizing that Jesus' burden is shared with us. As Jesus is led to Golgotha, the suffering He endures points to the immense love He has for humanity. This passage reminds us that following Jesus may come with burdens, but His sacrifice brings hope.

Bible Study Questions:

1. What significance does Simon's role play in showing that we all share in the journey of following Jesus?

2. How does witnessing Jesus' willingness to endure suffering affect your perspective on personal burdens?

3. What practical ways can you help carry the burdens of others in your community?

Application:
Consider a challenge or burden you're facing, and also think about someone else who might be struggling. Identify one small way to share encouragement or practical help, recognizing that we all need support along life's journey.

Prayer Focus:
"Lord, thank You for carrying the weight of our burdens. Help me to share Your love by supporting those who are struggling and to trust in Your redemptive purpose even in hardship. Amen."

DAY 4 OF MARK 15: THE AGONY OF THE CROSS

Scripture References: Mark 15:33–41

Theme:
As darkness falls over the land and Jesus hangs on the cross, we are confronted with the depth of His sacrifice. The dramatic events— from the cry of abandonment to the shaking of the earth—invite us to ponder the cost of redemption and the profound love behind it.

Bible Study Questions:

    1. What emotions do you think the witnesses felt as they

observed the events of the crucifixion?

2. How does the darkness and the cry of Jesus challenge your understanding of sacrifice and love?

3. In what ways can the suffering of Jesus inspire you to live more sacrificially for others?

Application:
Spend some quiet time today reflecting on the magnitude of Jesus' sacrifice. Consider writing a short journal entry on what His suffering means for you and how it might inspire you to serve others selflessly.

Prayer Focus:
"Jesus, thank You for enduring the darkness and pain out of love for me. Help me to understand the depth of Your sacrifice and live in a way that honors Your immense love. Amen."

DAY 5 OF MARK 15: THE COST AND PROMISE OF REDEMPTION

Scripture References: Mark 15:42–47

Theme:
Following Jesus' death, the narrative turns to His burial—a somber moment that also sets the stage for the promise of redemption. Joseph of Arimathea's act of care reminds us that even in death, there is hope for new beginnings through God's plan.

Bible Study Questions:

1. How does Joseph of Arimathea's compassion reflect the hope that can be found even in times of loss?

2. What does Jesus' burial teach you about the seriousness of His sacrifice and the promise of redemption?

3. In what ways can you embrace hope during periods of sorrow or despair?

Application:
Reflect on a time when you experienced loss or grief. Consider how the hope of redemption has played a role in your healing process. Think of one way to share that hope with someone who might be struggling with their own loss.

Prayer Focus:
"Lord, thank You for the promise of redemption even in the midst of sorrow. Help me to carry the hope of Your love into every dark place, trusting that new beginnings will come in Your time. Amen."

EXPLANATION OF MARK'S ORIGINAL ENDING (MARK 16:1-8) VS LONGER ENDING (MARK 16:9-20)

Mark likely ended at verse 8:

The earliest and most reliable copies of Mark's Gospel end with the women finding the empty tomb and running away in fear and amazement.

It's possible that Mark wanted the story to end this way to leave readers thinking, "What will we do with this news about Jesus?"

Verses 9-20 were probably added later:

Many scholars believe that later writers added these verses because they wanted to give the story a **clear ending**, similar to the Gospels of **Matthew, Luke, and John**, where Jesus appears to His followers after the resurrection.

How do we know it was added later?

The oldest copies of the Bible don't have these verses.

The writing style and word choice in verses 9-20 are very different from the rest of Mark's Gospel, which suggests it wasn't written by Mark.

Why are verses 9-20 still important to study?

These verses show important things about Jesus that match what we read in other Gospels:

Jesus appeared to His disciples.

He gave them a mission to **share the Good News** with the world.

He ascended into heaven and continues to guide us through the Holy Spirit.

What can we learn?

Even if these verses were added later, they teach powerful lessons:

1. Jesus is alive.
2. He wants us to share His love with others.
3. We can trust that Jesus' mission is still active today, and we're a part of it.

To wrap things up, it's likely that Mark originally ended at verse 8, and verses 9-20 were added later by someone else. While these added verses don't carry the same level of authority as the rest of Mark, they still offer valuable lessons and insights. That's why we've included them in our devotional—they can still encourage and guide us as we grow in our faith.

DAY 1 OF MARK 16: THE EMPTY TOMB —A MESSAGE OF NEW HOPE

Scripture References: Mark 16:1–8

Theme:
The discovery of the empty tomb marks the triumphant defeat of death. The women who went to the tomb found it empty, and an angel announced that Jesus had risen. This powerful message invites us to embrace hope and the promise of new life.

Bible Study Questions:

1. How does the sight of the empty tomb change your understanding of death and hope?

2. What feelings or thoughts arise when you consider that Jesus conquered death?

3. How can the promise of resurrection encourage you in moments of despair or loss?

Application:
Reflect on a time when you felt overwhelmed by despair or loss. Write down how the hope of resurrection could change your perspective, and consider sharing this hope with someone who might need encouragement.

Prayer Focus:
"Lord, thank You for the hope found in the empty tomb. Help me to embrace the new life You offer and to share that hope with others every day. Amen."

DAY 2 OF MARK 16: ENCOUNTERING THE RISEN CHRIST

Scripture References: Mark 16:9–11 *(Note: These verses appear in longer manuscript traditions.)*

Theme:
The early witnesses of the resurrection—those who encountered the risen Christ—offer us a personal invitation to experience His living presence. Their testimony inspires us to trust in His power and love.

Bible Study Questions:

1. What does it mean to you that Jesus is alive and present

in our lives today?

2. How can personal encounters with Christ transform your daily experience of faith?

3. In what ways can you be open to recognizing Jesus in the people and moments around you?

Application:
Think of a moment when you sensed God's presence or guidance in your life. Reflect on that experience and consider how you might be more attentive to His presence each day.

Prayer Focus:
"Jesus, thank You for rising and being alive among us. Open my eyes to Your presence in my daily life and help me trust in Your everlasting love. Amen."

DAY 3 OF MARK 16: THE GREAT COMMISSION— SHARING THE GOOD NEWS

Scripture References: Mark 16:15–18 *(Note: These verses appear in longer manuscript traditions.)*

Theme:
Jesus commands His followers to go into all the world and preach the gospel. This call is as relevant for us today as it was for the first disciples, reminding us that sharing the good news is

a vital part of our faith journey.

Bible Study Questions:

1. What does "preaching the gospel to every creature" mean for your life today?

2. How can sharing your personal experience of Jesus' love impact those around you?

3. What practical steps can you take to be more proactive in spreading the good news?

Application:

Identify one person or group in your community who might benefit from hearing about Jesus' love. Plan a simple, genuine way to share your faith—whether through conversation, a handwritten note, or social media.

Prayer Focus:

"Jesus, thank You for entrusting me with Your message. Give me the courage and creativity to share Your love and truth with everyone I meet. Amen."

DAY 4 OF MARK 16: SIGNS, WONDERS, AND THE POWER OF FAITH

Scripture References: Mark 16:17–18 *(Note: These verses appear in longer manuscript traditions.)*

Theme:
Jesus promises that believers will be empowered to perform signs and wonders as a testament to His resurrection. These verses remind us that God's power is active in our lives, encouraging us to live with bold, unwavering faith.

Bible Study Questions:

1. What do these promises of signs and wonders reveal about the power available to believers?

2. How have you experienced God's miraculous work in your own life or the lives of others?

3. In what ways can the assurance of God's power motivate you to live a more vibrant, courageous faith?

Application:
Reflect on a recent instance where you experienced or witnessed an unexpected blessing or miracle. Consider how that moment reinforced your trust in God's power, and share that story with someone who might need reassurance.

Prayer Focus:
"Lord, thank You for Your amazing power at work in my life. Strengthen my faith so that I may boldly rely on You and be a witness to Your miracles. Amen."

DAY 5 OF MARK 16: LIVING IN THE LIGHT OF RESURRECTION

Scripture References: Mark 16:19–20 *(Note: These verses appear in longer manuscript traditions.)*

Theme:
The final verses of Mark 16 remind us that after His resurrection, Jesus ascended into heaven, but He left us with a promise—He is with us always. This assurance empowers us to live confidently and joyfully, knowing that His resurrection transforms our everyday lives.

Bible Study Questions:

1. How does the promise of Jesus' constant presence influence your daily outlook and decisions?

2. What does it mean to "go out and preach" in the context of living a resurrected life?

3. In what practical ways can you embody the hope and joy of the resurrection in your relationships and community?

Application:
Review your daily routines and consider one change you can make that reflects the power and joy of the resurrection— whether it's a new habit of gratitude, an act of kindness, or an open invitation to others to join you in fellowship.

Prayer Focus:
"Jesus, thank You for being with me every day. Help me live boldly in the light of Your resurrection, sharing hope, joy, and love with everyone I encounter. Amen."

EPILOGUE

Congratulations on finishing the book of Mark! I pray that going through this material has deepened your love for God's Word. If you haven't yet, I highly encourage you to read through the other Gospel books as well: Matthew, Luke, and John. Each one offers a unique perspective on the life of Christ, and reading them together will give you a clearer understanding of His life and, hopefully, a deeper love for Jesus—the God-man who sacrificed His life to save us all from eternal destruction.

There is no greater story than the story of Jesus Christ found in the Gospels. May you continue to grow into the man or woman God designed you to be, all for the glory of His Kingdom! Until the return of Christ, let us remain steadfast and encourage one another toward Christlikeness.

ABOUT THE AUTHOR

David Or

David is married to Ashley, and together they have three boys and a Goldendoodle named Abby. David is of Chinese descent but was raised in the Philippines.

Since 2014, David has served as the Youth Pastor at Frisco Community Bible Church in Frisco, Texas. He earned his Master of Theology degree with an emphasis in the New Testament from Dallas Theological Seminary.

Made in the USA
Coppell, TX
19 May 2025

49632811R00098